Ruth

GOD USES ORDINARY PEOPLE

Ruth

GOD USES ORDINARY PEOPLE

Rev. G. Wieske

Published by The Study
Box 445, Fergus, Ontario
Canada N1M 3E2

Ruth : God uses ordinary people
Garrelt Wieske

Copyright © The Study 2019

All rights reserved. No part of this publication may be reproduced, stored in a retrieval system, or transmitted in any form, or by any means, electronic, mechanical, photocopying, recording or otherwise, without prior written permission of the publisher.

Unless otherwise noted, all Scripture quotations in this book are taken from the New International Version (1984). Grand Rapids, MI: Zondervan Publishing House, 1984. Print.

Psalm selections refer to those found in the Book of Praise: Anglo-Genevan Psalter. Winnipeg, MB: Premier Printing, 2014. Print.Unless otherwise noted, all Scripture quotations in this book are taken from the New International Version (1984). Grand Rapids, MI: Zondervan Publishing House, 1984. Print.

Library and Archives Canada Cataloguing in Publication

Title: Ruth : God uses ordinary people / Garrelt Wieske.
Names: Wieske, G., 1938- author.
Identifiers: Canadiana (print) 20190105917 | Canadiana (ebook) 20190105933 | ISBN 9780886661175
 (softcover) | ISBN 9780886661182 (HTML)
Subjects: LCSH: Bible. Ruth—Commentaries.
Classification: LCC BS1315.53 .W54 2019 | DDC 222/.3507—dc23

Printed in Canada

Photography/Cover design: @vanveenjf

Published by The Study
Box 445, Fergus, Ontario
Canada N1M 3E2
www.thestudy-books.com

ISBN-13 978-0-88666-117-5

TABLE OF CONTENTS

Ruth 1	The Importance of Covenantal Living	7
Ruth 2	God Works Through Ordinary People	21
Ruth 3	The Lord Provides Redemption	35
Ruth 4	The Glorious Messianic Future	49
	Prayer Before Your Bible Study	63
	Prayer After Your Bible Study	65

Ruth 1

The Importance of Covenantal Living

Additional reading: Deuteronomy 11:8-21

Suggested singing: Ps. 105:2,3,4; Ps. 128:1-3

Is the book of Ruth still relevant today? How can we benefit from a short book about ordinary people doing ordinary things thousands of years ago? Is all the talk about their day to day life with its hopes and disappointments, joys and sorrows, simply an introduction to the key event, a Moabite girl becoming the great-grandmother of King David and an ancestor of our Lord Jesus Christ? Certainly not. Reading through the book of Ruth, we can see that the first three chapters prepare us for the joyful news of the final chapter. That doesn't mean the message of this book is confined to Ruth becoming a mother of Jesus Christ. At the beginning already the Lord teaches us the importance of covenantal living, and shows us what happens if that is forgotten or ignored.

We tend to think that important and decisive events are the result of what great people accomplish, or fail to accomplish. The high and the mighty, the famous and powerful, *they* make an impact on the course of history! But we, common folk, pass through barely causing a ripple. The book of Ruth shows how wrong that thinking is, and highlights how important the actions of ordinary people are. It focuses particularly on how these actions impact the future of the Lord's kingdom and church.

Ruth relates that the effect of an individual's choices cannot be contained to that individual's life. It tells us that the road on which parents walk is, as a rule, also the road on which their children travel. Lest we despair, the book also reveals that the Lord is merciful and gracious. He comes to the aid of his people, sometimes in surprising and unexpected ways. But we may never use that as an excuse to forsake our covenantal responsibilities.

The Bible contains many examples of ordinary and unimportant people whose covenant obedience led to astounding results. The young and unnamed girl of 2 Kings 5:1-3 was instrumental in causing the pagan Naaman to give glory to the God of Israel after his miraculous recovery from leprosy. An elderly couple, observing all the commandments of God blamelessly, became the parents of John the Baptist who prepared the way of the Lord. Lois and Eunice, two women who loved the Lord, were used by him in such a way that the young boy Timothy became a faithful helper of the apostle Paul and a great blessing for the young churches of the New Testament.

We sometimes wonder what *we* are able to do for the Lord and his church. Life can be so ordinary and tedious even. We go through our daily routines and are busy with many necessary things. But we often fail to see how these matters relate to God and his service. Here the book of Ruth comes to our aid. We learn that the Lord doesn't expect us to set the world on fire, but wants us to live close to him - whether we are married or single, whether we are young or old, have children or not, prosperous or struggling to make ends meet. In the kingdom of God, it's faithfulness that counts. That primarily begins in those ordinary matters that govern our life. When we live out of God's covenant promises he will bless us and cause us *to be* a blessing. But when we take life in our own hands, everything goes from bad to worse.

There are no promises in the Bible that state the Lord will always come to the rescue of his children. It is pure grace that he does in the case of Elimelech's family. This outline focuses on how the Lord miraculously assures the future of his church despite the covenantal disobedience of Elimelech's family.

Departure from the Promised Land

"In the days when the judges ruled, there was a famine in the land." This sentence is not intended to indicate the *time period* so much as the *circumstances* in which God's people were living. From the book of Judges we know that when the judges ruled, God's people were living in blatant disobedience most of the time. They served the gods of their pagan neighbours, and participated in gross immorality. It's not a coincidence that in the last chapters of the book of Judges we read three times: "Israel had no King; everyone did as he saw fit."(e.g. Judges 21:25) The Lord was not acknowledged. There was no trust in him, and no desire to walk in his ways. It was under those circumstances that Elimelech and his family decided to leave Canaan.

Elimelech took his family to Moab. It was not all that far away, about a three-day journey. And so he left Bethlehem, his ancestral city, to seek his fortunes outside of the Promised Land. From the Hebrew, it is clear that Elimelech did not plan to stay in Moab, but intended to return. His main concern was to escape the famine and its hardships: the lack of food and depressed economy. Isn't that reasonable? After all, the Bible teaches that a believer who doesn't look after his family has denied the faith and is worse than an unbeliever (1 Timothy 5:8). In our time people emigrate or temporarily move away to take better care of their families. Is there anything wrong with that – provided, of course, that they don't forget the Lord and his church?

It is important to remember that we are speaking here of Old Testament times. God's people weren't spread across this world yet; his church was still confined to the nation of Israel. That nation occupied the Promised Land as its special possession and divine inheritance! The Lord dwelt in their midst. He had promised to take care of them because of his covenant. And *that's* why the famine was not an *ordinary* famine. God had promised Israel they would never suffer a famine, as long as they served him. They would always have plenty to eat, as long as they walked in his ways. Famines would only occur when they turned their back on the Lord and lived as the other nations, serving other gods (Deuteronomy 28:22).

Our chapter does not tell us why Elimelech left. It simply relates what happened to him and his sons during the next ten years. But when we compare Scripture with Scripture we know a famine in Palestine meant no food. Staying alive, therefore, required a move to another country. In his considerations, however, Elimelech forgot that the Lord had not made any covenant promises in Moab, as he had in Canaan. He neglected to ask why that famine had come and did not consider how to respond to the hardship in a God-pleasing way. He must have thought: "What do you do with God's promises when they aren't fulfilled? I must assure my family's wellbeing, and that requires a drastic move."

In Israel, names had great meaning. *Elimelech* means "God is my King". If he had lived up to his name, Elimelech would have stayed in Bethlehem. Ironically, *Bethlehem* means "house of bread". Elimelech should have said to himself: "*House of bread?* With nothing to eat? Why do we suffer scarcity when God has promised abundance?"

Instead of asking those questions, Elimelech used his "common sense". How often don't *we* do exactly the same? We know God's covenant promises. We've been assured that the Lord will always provide for our needs. But when things get difficult, we decide to do something about it ourselves. Now the Lord certainly doesn't want us to run away from our responsibilities. But "doing something" should not cause us to forsake God's covenant. It should not cause us to behave contrary to his Word. For faith is more than *knowing* God's promises - faith is revealed when we *live* them! When our choices and decisions are made based on them.

We cannot control the difficulties and hardships of life, but we are able to decide how to respond to them. We must respond in a God-pleasing way. That's what Elimelech *should* have done. He should have humbled himself! He should have said:

> Lord, we know that this famine is our own fault! For your people are living in sin. They don't *trust* you anymore. They want to determine their own life. That's why we have incurred your righteous anger. Have mercy on us, Lord! Remember your promises to take care of us. Please turn your anger away, and help us walk in the way of your Word.

Then God would have looked after this family even during famine because that's what he had *promised*! God always fulfills his promises, but Elimelech tried to solve his problems in his own way. He *left* the Promised Land. He took leave of the country to which God's blessings were confined. He thought he could assure his livelihood by being realistic, but he wasn't realistic at all. He was disobedient!

There's certainly a great difference between Elimelech's time and our time. We mentioned it already. God's church is no longer confined to one nation and his blessings no longer assure us of material prosperity. Many of God's people suffer want. A lot of his children are deprived of the abundance which Israel could claim in the land of Canaan. What has *not* changed is the call to *trust* in the Lord, by living within the covenant. When times are tough, do not look for ways and means that seem to make your life a lot easier but come at the price of disobeying God. For look what happened to Elimelech and his family. Instead of *escaping* death, they walked right into it. And not only physically, though that happened too! Ruth 1 tells us that not long after Elimelech left, he died. But what's worse, his sons fall in love with two Moabite girls and marry them.

Do you see what happens when the Lord is no longer trusted and you take life in your own hands? The commentators make much of the fact that Deuteronomy 7 does not prohibit Israel from marry Moabites - only the nations that lived in Canaan are forbidden. But does that mean that the Lord approved of Mahlon and Kilion's marriage? No. The Lord wants his people to marry in the unity of faith. How else are they able to serve him together and nurture their children in his ways? It's only because the original inhabitants of Canaan presented the greatest danger for intermarriage that the Lord lists them by name. Why else are Moabites not allowed to enter the tabernacle until the 10th generation? Why else was King Solomon later on faulted for marrying foreign women, many of whom were Moabites?

And so Elimelech's departure from the Promised Land spelled nothing but trouble and judgment, for he made light of God's covenant. If the Lord had not graciously intervened, his family would have perished in the wickedness of a false religion. That's why Elimelech's death wasn't accidental. Nor the childlessness of Mahlon and Kilion and their death at a rather young age. For you can't take liberties with the Lord and his covenant. It's a serious matter when you go your own way. Even when you do it with pious talk, like Elimelech might have done: "I'm not going to stay in Moab *forever*! When things pick up I'll go back." But he did not trust in the Lord. He doubted God's faithfulness. He put the material well being of his family *before* his submission to the God of the covenant. And that's why the Lord was against him. That's why they died! No, not in the sense that they were lost forever; the text doesn't mention that. But if it hadn't been for God's grace, Elimelech's family would have drowned in its covenant disobedience and missed out on the glorious future of God's church.

Return to Promised Land

After the death of Elimelech and his two sons, Naomi is left by herself. Sure, she has her two daughters-in-law, but they are strangers to God's covenant. Family ties are precious and when the unity of faith is missing they leave much to be desired. Those ties can never give you the joy that comes from serving the Lord together. Naomi has heard that the famine is over. The Lord in his mercy came to the aid of his children so that there is plenty of food again. And so she gathers her most important possessions and prepares to go back to Bethlehem. Back to the Promised Land. Back to her own people, accompanied by Orpah and Ruth.

While they are travelling she does her utmost to persuade the girls to remain in Moab. "Why don't you go back to your mother's home?" she asks. Why does Naomi do that? The text doesn't say, but it is likely that Naomi saw no future for Orpah and Ruth in Canaan. Does she realize that pagan girls can't expect to marry Israelite men, least of all in the Promised Land? She may also have been afraid that looking after 3 persons would be a lot harder than if she returned by herself. Whatever her deepest reasons, Naomi wishes them the blessing of the Lord. She hopes that the God of Israel will deal mercifully with them, just as they dealt with their husbands and with her. It shows us that these girls had really become part of Elimelech's family and that they loved it. They may not have broken with their past altogether but they felt very much at home with Naomi.

But Naomi has more to say. She also prays that the Lord might give them rest in the home of a new husband. How could she say *that*? Didn't she know that true rest can only be found in the Promised Land? Hadn't she learned *anything* from what had happened? What else had they encountered but unrest and sorrow? How can Naomi so casually suggest, "Go home and may the Lord give you rest?" It tells us that her sojourn in Moab had not been beneficial for her faith. That's what happens when you leave the ways of the Lord and follow your own heart. Your faith convictions start to erode and you begin to compromise. Eventually you fall away from the faith altogether, if God doesn't graciously prevent it.

The girls *refuse* to return. They become upset and say, "We won't go back, but we will go with you to your people." Naomi doesn't give up. This time she paints a very bleak picture of their future. "I'm too old to have any more sons," she says. "And even if I had a husband, even if I became pregnant tonight, would you wait for my sons to grow up? Would you be willing to remain single until they were men? Come on, girls, be sensible. This won't work. Think of your future!" she continues. All this may sound a little strange to our ears but Naomi refers to what God had said in Deuteronomy 25, where the brother of a man who had died without children was to marry his widow. Then, the first child of that marriage was to carry on the name of the deceased. Feminism proclaims that independence and pursuing a career is the height of happiness for a woman, and children are often not wanted. But in the days of Ruth a good marriage provided security and satisfaction which a girl couldn't find anywhere else.

Naomi's last remark is the worst. "It may not be easy for *you*," she says, "but it's *a lot* harder for *me*. For the Lord's hand is against me!" In other words, she blames God for her troubles. Did she not see that her troubles were a result of their departure from the Promised Land? Of their failure to trust the Lord? That's what happens when we try to safeguard our own life. Then we reason from the facts instead of from God's promises. That never works - sooner or later we have to face the consequences. The Lord will be against us. For his *blessing* doesn't rest on us and *without* his blessing there is no future.

Orpah is finally persuaded. She kisses her mother-in-law goodbye and goes back. Back to what? Not only to her country but also to the religion of Moab – at Naomi's advice! We shouldn't be too hard on Orpah, as if she defiantly rebels against Israel's God. True, by returning she rejects the Lord, but she doesn't know any better. No, that doesn't excuse her, but let's not forget that she had not been exposed to the gospel and its blessings as *we* have. In Elimelech's family she no doubt heard about the Lord, but she didn't witness how important he was. What can you expect, especially when your own mother-in-law suggests you had better go home?

Ruth refuses to go. She clings even closer to her mother-in-law. But Naomi doesn't relent. "Go back with Orpah," she says. "Back to your own people and your own gods!" Isn't that terrible, sending your relatives to eternal damnation? For the gods of Moab are false gods! Idols who are unable to save people from their greatest misery, which is God's terrible wrath on sin. There's salvation only with the God of Israel, and only in the Promised Land is there forgiveness, the ministry of reconciliation. Only the church of the Lord has a future. *That's* what Naomi should have said! It shows us how far she has strayed from the ways of the Lord.

But Ruth can't be swayed. "I'm going with you," she says. "There's no point trying to dissuade me. I've made up my mind!" And then she speaks those well-known words: "Your people will be my people and your God will be my God. I'll stay where you stay and where you die I will die and there I will be buried!" Was this a confession of faith? Had Ruth become a believer in the God of Israel? It sure sounds like it. And she's not finished yet. She swears an oath! She calls God by his covenant name. LORD! The God who doesn't change. The God who remains faithful to what he has promised. Isn't this incredible? How could this pagan girl make such a profession? What made her willing to leave her native land, her family and her religion and stay with Naomi until death?

This was the Lord's doing, not Naomi's. Sure, we have no reason to believe that Elimelech and his family had written God off completely. They would have talked about him from time to time, because how else could Ruth have come to know of him? How *much* she heard, we don't know, and how much she *understood*, we know even less. But her mother-in-law sure didn't witness that the God of Israel and his covenant promises were most important in Elimelech's family! That's why all praise goes to the Lord. It is *he* who prepares Ruth's heart for the gospel, while Orpah's heart remains closed. He has mercy on this heathen girl, because he is busy with the future of his church. A future which Elimelech's family jeopardized by their covenantal disobedience.

Naomi *should* have shown that mercy and compassion! For God had made provisions that also strangers could be incorporated into his covenant people. But if Naomi had had her way, both Orpah *and* Ruth would have perished in their sins. That's what happens when you blame the Lord for your troubles and no longer trust him, instead going your own way. There are millions of Orpahs who never witness in God's children the joy and thankfulness that belonging to the Lord should bring. Though that's not an excuse to reject him, don't be surprised that others aren't drawn to the Lord and his church if *we* don't show that we love God's promises and cling to them in good and bad times,

And what about the thousands of Ruths who have come to know the Lord? Are they the product of *our* faithfulness and commitment? No way! It's by God's grace they came to faith. Often not *because of* but *despite* the lifestyle of God's people. This does not mean that our commitment is irrelevant. God *will* bring to faith all whom he has chosen. He *will* build his church, but he normally uses *our* faithfulness. That's the way he has revealed in his Word. Our call is to walk in God's way, and to love the Lord and to trust that he will provide even in difficult times. That's how the Lord extends his covenant blessings from generation to generation. That's how God-fearing parents will see their children grow up to love him. And that's how God adds to his people those who did not know him before.

At last Naomi gives in. She realizes that Ruth is determined to go with her. And so the two of them continue on their journey. Mother and daughter-in-law, both of them widows. Both of them with no future, humanly speaking. But the Lord has other plans; his mercy is unfathomable. We see that especially as they arrive in the Promised Land.

Arrival in the Promised Land

When they enter Bethlehem there's a buzz of excitement. Word spreads quickly that Naomi has returned and all the women come out to meet her. Apparently they haven't forgotten her yet. Though ten years older, they recognize her. "Is it really you, Naomi?" they ask. Implied is the question, "What happened? Where is your husband? And where are your boys?"

Naomi doesn't leave them guessing. "Don't call me Naomi any longer but call me Mara," she says, "because the Lord has made my life very bitter! I went away full but look how I'm coming back – I've got nothing left! My husband and sons are gone and it's all the Lord's doing. He has afflicted me. He is the cause of my misfortune!" That is what often happens when God's children meet with adversity and sorrow. They don't wonder whether *they* might be the cause of it but they put the blame somewhere else, even on God. The name *Naomi* means "pleasantness" or "loveliness", while *Mara* means "bitterness". "Well," says Naomi, "my name was a big mistake. There's nothing pleasant anymore. There's only bitterness!" But is that true? Does Naomi evaluate the situation properly? No.

First of all she exaggerates. Sure, she had a husband and children when they left, but had she forgotten *why* they went to Moab? If their life was so full, why did they leave? Weren't they dissatisfied? Did they not go away because they wanted a more prosperous life? And even more important to ask is: when is your life exactly "full"? When you've got your family and plenty to eat? Is *that* what the covenant stands for? What about the Lord? What about his blessings of forgiveness and love? Are they not the greatest treasures of God's people? Is there anyone or anything that is more important than the Lord and his service?

But there's more yet. Was Naomi right in ascribing her afflictions to the Lord? Sure, in one way she was right, for the Lord reigns! There's nothing that happens by chance. God is in full control, also of the lives of his people. That's why Elimelech's death and the death of his sons didn't just happen. They were determined by God, and the fact that Naomi returned as a poor widow was *also* his doing ultimately. That does not mean that God can be blamed for our sorrows and afflictions; people have their own responsibility. Though the Lord is in control, the results of our sin cannot be passed onto him. That's our own doing.

That's what Naomi does not acknowledge. She's so immersed in self-pity and so upset about all she went through, that she accuses the Lord. He is the cause of all her troubles. She completely ignores her own accountability and she has no eye for God's *mercy*. That's what carries the day, lighting the darkness brought about by Elimelech's covenant unfaithfulness. We see that light not only in that the Lord brings Naomi back but that Ruth comes with her. Ruth, the Moabite and one-time pagan who came to trust in the God of Israel and who wanted to go to the Promised Land at any price. Ruth has begun to see what Naomi did not see yet, that only in Canaan would God's children be safe and secure - even when there was a famine. For that is where God's covenant blessings are given and enjoyed, and the Messiah was promised.

Today, God's promises are no longer restricted to one nation, and the Promised Land is not a country but the new creation. The blessings of the covenant have become much greater and far more profound because of our Lord Jesus Christ. Ever since he died and rose from the dead, he stands as guarantor that the Lord takes care of his children, in every respect. But we need to put him first, and have covenantal obedience. If that is denied, ignored, or forgotten, we will get enmeshed in our own solutions and the Lord will be against us because of that disobedience.

We started this study by stressing the importance of covenantal living. The future of the church is shaped and determined by ordinary people like you and me. When fathers and mothers go about their daily work in dependence on God, when our children are instructed in the fear of the Lord, when we're busy with many things but in those things reflect our love for our Heavenly Father, generations will be blessed. If we put our own desires before the will of God, if we try to secure our safety while violating our covenant obligations, our children and grandchildren will turn away from the Lord altogether and congregations will cease to be faithful.

Elimelech's entire family would have perished, if it hadn't been for God's compassion. It was not Naomi's doing that everything turned out well. It was the Lord's miraculous intervention. He wanted to use these two women for the coming of the Lord Jesus Christ! That was and that *still* is the reason why the future of the church is assured. Our text says that the barley harvest was just beginning. It was spring! Barley was the first crop that was reaped. In other words, it was the start of a new season. A season of life and growth, of harvest and plenty. That "new season" wasn't limited to the agricultural realm, for the following chapters tell us how God prepared the throne of David, from whom the Christ would be born, as King over his church. Through Ruth, God assured the future of Naomi's family and of the people of Israel, and thus of the entire catholic church to which we also may belong.

That's why our life is so safe and secure when we live in covenant with God. Then we do not have to fear the troubles and afflictions we meet, for the Lord will watch over his church, as he has done during its long history. Christ has come to redeem his people. He now rules as King over all and he has promised that he will be with us until the end of this age. That's why you can be busy living out of God's promises. Knowing that your labour in the Lord is not in vain, you will realize he wants to use you for the coming of Christ's glorious kingdom in your job, your business, your home, your school, in your family life, nurturing your children, or in your retirement!

Questions

1. In Ruth 1 the nation of Israel was visited with a famine. We believe that "all things come not by chance, but from God's Fatherly hand" (HC, LD 1, Q&A 1). That means also today calamity strikes our nation with God's permission. How, then, do we interpret natural disasters? Are they a call to repentance from unbelief? God's judgment for unfaithfulness?

2. How is the move of Elimelech's family to Moab different than the Dutch immigration to Canada in the 1950s?

    How is it the same?

3. Elimelech chose to leave the Promised Land. Was he then also leaving God's covenant?

4. Not all of our actions will "change the world", but how can our faithfulness in daily tasks influence the world?

5. Discuss how those dismissed by the world (e.g. the elderly, the handicapped, stay-at-home moms) play an important role in society.

_____
_____
_____

6. Give 2 biblical examples (other than Ruth) of how everyday actions have far-reaching impact.

_____
_____
_____

   Give 2 modern examples of everyday actions having far-reaching impact.

_____
_____
_____

7. What is Naomi's attitude and situation when she returns to Bethlehem?

_____
_____
_____
_____

   Was Naomi right in ascribing her afflictions to God?

_____
_____
_____

8. How does Ruth and Naomi's return to the Promised Land fit in with God's covenantal requirement of obedience?

_____
_____
_____
_____

How does their return fit in with the promises of a Messiah?

_____
_____
_____

9. Discuss 1 Timothy 5:8: "If anyone does not provide for his relatives, and especially for his immediate family, he has denied the faith and is worse than an unbeliever." In what circumstances was this statement made?

_____
_____
_____

Would it have applied to Elimelech while in Israel? ... in Moab?

_____
_____
_____

Does it apply to us today? If so, how?

_____
_____
_____

Are there situations in which it is acceptable to deny assistance to blood and church family members?

_____
_____
_____

RUTH 2

GOD WORKS THROUGH ORDINARY PEOPLE

Additional Reading: Leviticus 23:22 and Deuteronomy 24:14-22

Suggested singing: Psalm 63: 2,3; Hymn 78:1,2,5

The Lord usually works out his purposes in and through the ordinary and everyday activities of his people. We tend to think that breathtaking events and extraordinary achievements are the means God wants to use. Of course, there are times that the Lord calls certain men and women to accomplish almost superhuman tasks and unusual feats of faith, but God's normal way of working out his purpose is when we are faithful in whatever he calls us to do. Fathers who go to work each day, mothers that look after their families, boys and girls that go to school or college, and our elderly brothers and sisters who are enjoying their retirement are all called to live their life in and for the Lord. When we do that, when we are faithful in our daily pursuits, we may trust that we serve God's glory and the coming of his kingdom.

It's the *Lord* who builds his church and who directs everything to come to the fulfilment of his promises. He does that either through us or without us, for his counsel will stand and he fulfills all his purposes! Elimelech and his family took matters in their own hand. They did not live by faith but tried to secure their wellbeing by going to Moab, to escape the famine and so to assure their future. But what a disaster that turned out to be! If it hadn't been for God's covenant faithfulness and grace, the family would have perished in their disobedience. But the Lord had other plans. He brought Naomi and Ruth back to the Promised Land, for he wanted to use this family for the coming of his Son, the promised Messiah, who was to be born from the tribe of Judah and whose ancestors were to become kings in Israel. The coming of that Son is the main theme of the book of Ruth.

That's why Elimelech's family doesn't drown in covenantal disobedience but becomes a building block in the family tree of our Saviour, and that is what our chapter prepares us for. Oh, the miraculous ways of the Lord! Naomi and Ruth came back to Bethlehem, poor and bereft. How will things proceed? What does the future have in store for these two widows - an elderly woman and a Moabite girl? One who is bitter and blames God for her misfortune and the other a stranger to God's covenant? Humanly speaking, it doesn't look good at all. The Lord has great surprises in store for them, however. He wants to use this family for the establishment of the Messianic kingship. From the darkness that prevailed in the time of the Judges, God is busy ensuring that the light of the world may arrive. He is busy so that his promise to Abraham is realized, and *all* the peoples of the earth will be blessed *through him*. He is also busy ensuring that Jacob's blessing to Judah will be fulfilled: "The scepter will not depart from Judah, nor the ruler's staff from between his feet, until he comes to whom it belongs and the obedience of the nations is his." (Gen. 49:10)

Do you hear the worldwide implications of these promises? Do you realize that the Messiah will not only be the King of Israel but of *all* the nations? That's why Ruth, in becoming a member of God's Old Testament people, gives us a foretaste of what Pentecost will usher in. Her faith in Israel's God is the prelude to that innumerable multitude from every nation that put their trust in the Saviour of the world.

The three main characters in this chapter don't have a clue about that. Ruth, Boaz and Naomi are people of their time; they have a limited vision and no inkling of what God is going to accomplish through them. Yet through their simple faith, covenantal obedience, and true repentance, the Lord brings closer the Day of Jesus Christ - Christmas. In this way a people will be redeemed, not just from Israel but from every tribe and tongue; God's catholic church will sing his praise into all eternity.

This second outline focuses on how the Lord prepares Elimelech's family for the coming of his kingdom.

The Faith of Ruth

It is important to remember that the book of Ruth is an appendix to the book of Judges. At that time things were very bad. Israel lived in gross apostasy and terrible sin. "In those days Israel had no king; everyone did as he saw fit." (Judges 17:5; 21:25) There was no one who ruled the nation in the ways of the Lord. Moses was long gone and so was Joshua. There was no central authority which shepherded Israel in the service of God. The people followed their own heart. Yes, there were exceptions. Even during the time of the Judges the Lord had his children who did not follow the majority in their pursuit of evil and wickedness. Boaz was one of them. But the main purpose of the book of Ruth is not to offset the many sad stories found in Judges with a happy one.

The Bible does not just tell us stories. The Word of God is not primarily interested in our emotional needs. Rather, it is the revelation of God's grace! A grace that takes care of our deepest needs. The book of Ruth proclaims that no matter how dark it gets, the Lord does not forsake his covenant promises. He is always busy bringing about the deliverance of his people. Freedom not only from enemies of flesh and blood but especially from our greatest enemies: Satan, sin, and our own depraved nature. That already becomes evident from the first verse of the second chapter where we are introduced to Boaz.

For what is emphasized in that first verse? That this man is a relative of Naomi *on her husband's side*, from the clan of Elimelech. He also is a man of standing. A prosperous farmer and a well-to-do businessman. The fact that he is a wealthy relative sets the tone of the rest of the book, because it reminds us of what the Lord is after. He wants to use Elimelech's family for the coming of Jesus Christ. Boaz' relationship to Naomi and his prosperity are the means God uses to assure the continuation of Elimelech's family, which belongs to the tribe of Judah. And so the Lord prepares the throne of David, the illustrious forefather of Jesus Christ. The Lord is preparing a kingdom that will eventually span the entire world and all who trust in him as their Saviour and Lord will belong to it!

Now let us consider the events of this chapter and their importance for what God is going to perform. How does the Lord prepare for this kingdom? Should we expect to read of extraordinary events? Breathtaking accomplishments? No, God prepares using common and ordinary means.

The trusting faith of Ruth is the first thing God uses. Naomi and her daughter-in-law have to make a living. You can't survive without food and drink. That is why Ruth says, "Naomi, let me go to the fields and pick up the leftover grain behind anyone in whose eyes I find favor." That was quite something, for Ruth was a stranger. She was not aware of the customs of the land. How would she have known that the Lord had made provisions in his law for the poor to make ends meet? Doesn't that tell us that she must have spoken about these matters with Naomi, asking her how to proceed with no food and no income?

Notice that *Ruth* takes the initiative, and Naomi does not have to push her. We don't read that she says to Ruth, "Well girl, it's about time you *do* something! We've got to eat, you know!" Ruth volunteers to go. Let's not overlook that, saying,

> "What's the big deal? Of course, Ruth knew just as well as Naomi that the pantry was empty and that something had to be done to fill their stomachs. Since Naomi was an elderly woman, isn't it logical that the younger one takes it on herself to go out and work for a living?"

But if we reason like that, we minimize the fact that she was an alien. A non-Israelite. Hardly anyone knew her. How would she be received? How would the people treat her? Especially since she was a young female. The later references that the men should not molest her speak for themselves. She was "easy pickings", you might say. She didn't know anyone who could protect her.

But even *more* important, what if Ruth had said to Naomi:

> Hey, where is that God of yours who will care for his people? Didn't you tell me that Canaan is the Promised Land? Didn't you say more than once that you and your family should have never left Palestine since God's blessings are confined to it? Where are those blessings now, Naomi? We've been here for some time now but I haven't *noticed* any yet.

But Ruth doesn't talk like that at all. She doesn't complain and feel sorry for herself and her mother-in-law. She neither blames God nor demands he take care of them. She is willing to go to work. Not for eight hours a day in an air conditioned office, but from dawn to dusk doing backbreaking work, with the risk of being ill-treated and receiving very little, if anything, in return. And *that* shows us her faith. That tells us this Moabite girl, this stranger in a strange land, has used her time well. Her profession of faith mentioned in the previous chapter - that Naomi's people would be her people and Naomi's God would be her God - was not said on the spur of the moment. It came from her heart. The Lord had worked this faith in her. He also used Naomi's conversations with Ruth about how the poor were to be provided for, as laid down in his law, to make her realize that his promises do not exempt us from the call to work for a living.

That's why Ruth goes! She trusts in Israel's God. She believes that he won't disappoint her. And he doesn't; the Lord never disappoints those who trust in him and live by faith. For look what happens! With Naomi's approval she sets out on her unknown journey. Where will she end up? How will it go? Will the people allow her to reap or will they tell her to get lost? For let us not forget that we are dealing with the time of the Judges, when the great majority have no time for God's laws and almost everyone is out for himself. The fact that God instructed the farmers not to harvest the edges of their fields but to leave that for the poor and the foreigners did not mean that this was always done. If many Israelites violated the most important of God's commandments why should we expect them to keep the lesser ones?

But the Lord is with Ruth. "As it turned out" (Ruth 2:3) she found herself in a field belonging to Boaz. (Note the addition: "Who was from the clan of Elimelech", for this will play an important role in the future of Naomi and Ruth.) "As it turned out." That's the way *we* speak and even the Bible does not refrain from using it. But this was God's providence! This was the way the Lord blessed the simple faith of this new and young believer. He is in charge of everything. If not even one hair falls from our head without his will, then absolutely nothing happens by chance. It was the Lord's hand that guided Ruth's steps. It was *his* doing that her faith was not put to shame. The farms in those days were not marked by fences nor were their owner's names displayed. As a rule, the fields were all joined together and only some stones served as boundary markers. How remarkable! We see God at work here, preparing Ruth for what he has in mind. Busy with Naomi's family which he wants to use for the coming of his kingdom.

That hasn't changed. Today also the Lord asks nothing more of us than to be faithful in our daily task. Let us never forget that or fall into the trap of believing that "working for the Lord" only means being a missionary or devoting yourself exclusively to spiritual matters. The Lord wants us to live before him in trusting faith. In Ruth's case we see God's work as part of his redemptive purpose, bringing about the coming of his kingdom and the incarnation of his Son. In *our* time God works toward the second coming of Christ, in and through our faithful involvement in our daily calling. He wants to use you as you go about your daily activities. The Lord is pleased when we work hard at our daily calling, whatever that may be, and wherever that brings us: school, home, or the workplace.

Ruth worked with zeal, and the Lord blessed that. The rest of the chapter makes that very clear. When Boaz turns up, he takes a genuine interest in Ruth. He tells her not to go anywhere else and ensures she is treated as one of Boaz' workers. What a comfort for this Moabite girl! What a blessing the God of Israel gives her. When at last the day is past and Ruth heads home, tired but very happy, she's got an ephah of barley. Enough to eat for a whole week for the two of them. Far, far more than a normal day of gleaning would produce. She can't keep quiet about her experiences. She tells Naomi everything. And she's allowed to stay at Boaz' farm until the end of the barley and wheat harvest.

Do you see, how the Lord uses this Moabite girl to fulfill his plan? How he blessed her trusting faith to achieve what he had in mind? True, Ruth did not know that yet. Apart from Naomi's reference to Boaz being one of their kinsman redeemers, the future is a closed book for Ruth. She has no clue what the Lord has in store for her. But that's not most important right now. This is: Ruth's simple and trusting faith has been richly rewarded.

The Lord has been so good to her, and it's *that* truth that will also take care of what the future will bring. Just as with us. We do not know what the Lord has in store for *us*. *We* must live by faith, one day at a time, too. When we do so, by the grace of God, and simply live in love and obedience to our faithful Father in our day to day life, we will experience his blessings. Then he will also use us to hasten the Day of his Son.

The Compassion of Boaz

God uses Boaz' compassion to prepare Elimelech's family for the coming of his kingdom. Boaz pays a visit to his workers to see how the work is progressing. "The Lord be with you!" he says. What a beautiful way of greeting your employees! There are commentators who say: "This is just a worn-out cliché. You shouldn't read too much into it." But if that were the case, why would the Bible mention it? No, it tells us that this man is an Israelite who loves God, and his workers know that. They answer him with, "The Lord bless you!" But then Boaz notices Ruth. "Who's that?" he asks. "That's the Moabite girl who came back with Naomi," says his foreman. "She's been here since the break of day, after I gave her permission to glean on your field. And she's a good worker too! She's only taken a short rest."

Boaz is impressed. There's something about that girl that piques his interest. Was it the way she worked? No doubt, that was part of it. But Boaz' interest goes further. He's heard about this girl. He knows that she left Moab after the death of her husband to be with Naomi and to take care of her. She gave up her own family and went to a foreign land and to a people she didn't know. That was quite something! You don't meet people like that very often - most of them would have stayed in their own country, with their own people, and their own gods.

That's why Boaz tells her not to glean in any other field but to stay on his farm. He offers her protection as well. He tells his workers not to trouble Ruth with coarse jokes or harassment. He allows her to drink from the same water jars as his workers. When Ruth is taken aback by such generosity and compassion and asks why he's dealing with her – a stranger – with so much kindness, he says he's really impressed by Ruth's devotion. He prays that the Lord may repay her for all she has done. "May the God of Israel reward you richly, under whose wings you have sought refuge," he says. But even that isn't the end. At mealtime, Boaz calls Ruth to eat with his harvesters and personally offers her some roasted grain. When the work resumes, he orders his men to pull out some extra stalks for her and to let her glean *among* the sheaves. He also orders them to make sure that nobody scolds her for this.

Is this normal? Is this the manner God wanted the farmers to provide for the poor? No way! Boaz' compassion goes way beyond that. We read from Deuteronomy 24:21 that an overlooked sheaf should not be retrieved. And Leviticus 19:9 and 23:22 tell us that the very edges of a field should not be harvested and what is accidentally dropped by the reapers should not be gleaned. But nowhere does the law provide that the poor are to be allowed between the sheaves or that the harvesters should consciously pull out some stalks for them. This gives us a glimpse into the heart and mind of Boaz. He does not only stick to the letter of the law but he reveals its spirit, and so shows himself to be a true child of God.

Boaz is a man who knows his Bible and the history of his people. When he hears who Ruth is, and what she has done for Naomi, he completely forgets that she's a foreigner. Or rather, he is filled with compassion toward her. Just as the Lord is. For though Israel was God's covenant people, though the Lord had set his love upon this nation at the exclusion of all others, that does not mean that the Lord has no time for foreigners. On the contrary, there are many passages in the Old Testament where God demands that his people be merciful toward foreigners. He even allows them to become part of his people. His laws apply to them just as much as to the Israelites (Lev. 24:22). That's why he said, "Do not oppress an alien; you yourselves know how it feels to be aliens, because you were aliens in Egypt" (Ex. 23:9).

It is this compassion, this realization that Ruth has taken refuge under the wings of Israel's God, which compels Boaz to treat her as he does. He does not act out of a sense of duty, or a need to obey the law. Today we meet many people who are careful to live according to the letter of God's law but who are foreign to its spirit. They are quite happy with themselves. They give to each what is due, but they are foreign to the concept of grace: they have no inkling that a man is saved not because of what *he* has done but because of what *Christ* has done. Oh, on the outside they are impeccable. They try to live a decent life, but have never seen themselves as being just as lost as everybody else and have never realized that salvation is the fruit of God's compassion only.

You are not a child of God simply because you obey the law. The most decent person can be just as far from the Lord as the most wicked sinner. It's only when God's grace has made you very small before him, that you realize that God wants your *heart*. And that's the case with Boaz! He knows that all his material and spiritual riches come from the gracious hand of his God. It's that knowledge that makes him so generous toward Ruth, whom he recognizes as a sister in the Lord. True, a foreigner, but brought near to the Lord because of God's love for this girl. A love that rests in his grace and can only be adored. It's this love that embraces all who belong to the Lord - whether Israelite or Moabite, white or black, rich or poor.

Here we witness how God's grace not only uses Ruth's simple faith but also Boaz' heartfelt compassion to prepare the coming of God's kingdom. He uses them to bring the Saviour to this world, as the great Son of King David. Before we see how this comes about, let us see what role Naomi plays.

The Repentance of Naomi

Naomi. Was this not the woman who said, "Call me Mara from now on, for my life is bitter because the Lord has afflicted me"? Yes, that's her, and God has not forgotten her. The Lord does not forsake his children the moment they get entangled in sin and rebellious thoughts. He seeks their repentance, and he often uses other people to bring that about (though repentance itself remains God's work). That's exactly what happens here, too. When Naomi hears what Ruth has experienced and where she worked, she realizes that this is not accidental, but belongs to God's providential care. All of a sudden she's struck by his covenant faithfulness. "Blessed is that man," she exclaims. Yes, the Lord bless him!

Naomi continues, "[The Lord] has not stopped showing his kindness to the living and the dead." What does she mean? "The living" refers to Naomi and Ruth. Now that there is food on the table and work for the future, Naomi recognizes the generous hand of God who takes care of them. But what about "the dead"? How does God show his kindness to them? To Elimelech and Mahlon, Ruth's deceased husband? They died in Moab. They perished outside the Promised Land. How can you show kindness to the *dead*? Through Boaz! For that name rings a bell in Naomi's mind. "He's our close relative," she says. "One of our kinsman-redeemers". And it's that fact which opens up the future. For a kinsman-redeemer is the man who assures the continuation of a family when the husband has passed away. The fact that Boaz is one of them is enough for Naomi to regain her hopes in God's kindness and faithfulness. And that's why she repents. That's why she sings of God's goodness toward her and Ruth, the living, and to Elimelech's and Mahlon's family as well. For though they have died, the kinsman-redeemer will rescue their family from extinction. The family line will carry on, so "the dead's" descendants will be there to welcome the Messiah.

And so everything comes together. What a difference from the end of chapter one! Then there was bitterness and poverty. The Lord was blamed for all their troubles. He afflicted them. But our chapter ends on a note of great hope. The bitterness is gone and poverty is a thing of the past. Now the future beckons. A future where a kinsman- redeemer will assure that all is not lost. A new era will dawn. At this particular time, everything is still hazy and indistinct. Ruth, Boaz and Naomi do not yet know how it will all turn out. But the Lord does, and let us not forget that he is at work here. He will see to it that Elimelech's name wasn't a misnomer. Elimelech means, "My God is King!" and that name will be vindicated. For the Lord is in a hurry. The throne of David will surely come, and the great Son of David will definitely arrive.

It will take centuries, and a lot needs to happen first. But already in our chapter Jesus Christ is at work as the promised Messiah. For he is the content of the entire Word of God. It is he who prepares his own coming into the flesh. Though he will be born *from* David, he is at the same time David's *Lord*. And that's how he is at work in this book. Ruth's faith was not of her own making, and neither was Boaz' compassion, nor Naomi's repentance. He, who once said, "Before Abraham was born, I am," (John 8:58) is busy bringing God's kingdom into the world. He can't wait for Christmas. For he has one ambition and that is to do his Father's will, saving a church to eternal life. A church, not only out of Israel but from every tribe, tongue and nation. He used Ruth, Boaz and Naomi for that glorious truth.

We are living so much later. The events in this book took place more than 3000 years ago. But they still speak to us. Oh yes, Christ *has* come, and Christmas was followed by Good Friday and Easter. The war has been won - the church has been ransomed. As our *Goel* (Hebrew for *Redeemer*), Christ laid down his life and set us free from the curse of God and the shackles of sin. What *hasn't* changed is the fact that also today he wants to use us to work out his purposes. In Ruth's time things looked very bleak for the church of God, and our own times don't promise much good either, humanly speaking. But the Lord is faithful. He's a complete Saviour. He takes care of all our needs. When we live in simple faith, when God's grace makes us compassionate toward our neighbour and we repent and rejoice in God's covenant faithfulness, the future lights up. Our hearts start to beat faster, for God's kingdom is coming. Our Lord is in a hurry, this time to return on the clouds of heaven, full of glory and of grace. He is keen to wrap us in his arms, press us to his bosom, to keep us with him forever. Therefore, lift up your heads, for your salvation is drawing near.

Questions

1. How is the book of Ruth a story about Christmas (Christ's incarnation)?

2. Ruth's faith leads her to work to provide for her mother-in-law. How was that an act of faith?

   Give some examples of acts of faith that we might perform in our daily life.

   How does God bless Ruth's faith?

3. How is Boaz Christ-like?

   To what degree does Boaz perform his work? For example, if you were to give him a performance review out of five, what would you give him?

   How do we see that God lives in Boaz' heart?

   How can we display this character in our daily life?

   Would you say that all elders should have the character of Boaz?

4. How has Naomi changed from chapter one to chapter two?

   What do you think happened to her to change her heart?

How is her change in heart obvious?

_____
_____
_____

5. Is it fair to say Naomi only repented because things got better for her?

   _____
   _____

   Looking in your own life, do you ever feel that you can only be happy when things get better?

   _____
   _____
   _____

   We are exhorted to be content in all circumstances (Philippians 4:12). How can we do that?

   _____
   _____
   _____

6. We confess that God works all things to the good of those who love him (Romans 8:28). How was this true for Naomi?

   _____
   _____
   _____

   How does knowing that God works this way affect how we respond to difficult circumstances?

   _____
   _____
   _____
   _____
   _____

How does knowing this comfort us when God sends hardship?

RUTH 3

THE LORD PROVIDES REDEMPTION FOR ELIMELECH'S FAMILY

Additional Reading: Leviticus 25:8-28; Deuteronomy 25:5-10; Revelation 21:1-5

Suggested singing: Psalm 19:3,6; Hymn 64:1,2

Did we read that right? Is Naomi encouraging Ruth to seduce Boaz, in order to trap him into marriage? Isn't that immoral? What does that have to do with the gospel of Jesus Christ? These and similar thoughts whirl through our minds when we read Ruth 3. But let's be careful, for also this event is part of the Word of God. Also here we are confronted with the truth that every part of Scripture is divinely inspired. This ought to make us cautious and not jump to wrong conclusions.

So why does God include these events in the Bible? Because he uses Naomi, Ruth, and Boaz to prepare for the coming of his Son! It is *he* who is at work here via people, and by means of their plans and actions. They are not as objectionable as we tend to think, but proceed from the customs and traditions of that time. Even more important, they are based on the covenantal rights and obligations which the Lord had given to his people. Yes, to us it all sounds very strange, and that's putting it mildly. Before we let our imagination run away, let's not forget that Boaz is an honourable man, who takes no offense at the manner in which Ruth approaches him. Ruth is a God-fearing woman of noble character as verse 11 tells us. Naomi, too, is a repentant child of God, who has been humbled by God's goodness. That's why we have to look in a different direction to understand what's going on here. That different direction is the law of our God and the legal provisions which the Lord laid down in it for the poor and widows.

We read about those provisions in Leviticus and Deuteronomy. There we find the key to what's happening here, so let's look at it a little closer. Israel was God's special people. He was their king and as such the land belonged to him. The Jews only enjoyed the use of it as their inheritance. If anyone was obliged to sell his property, because of poverty for example, then it was the duty of the nearest relative to redeem it. If that didn't happen, then the property would return to the original owner in the year of Jubilee, which came every 50th year. Consequently, no actual sale (as we understand it) took place. Rather, it was simply a sale of the yearly produce. The property had to stay within the family, so that no Israelite would remain poor.

The Lord had also instituted the levirate marriage. "Levir" is the Latin word for brother-in-law. If an Israelite man died without children, then his brother had the duty to take his widow as wife. The first child of this marriage would carry on the deceased man's name so that it did not become extinct in Israel. This son also became the legal heir of the property that belonged to the deceased. Although this law only applied to the brothers of the deceased, in the time of our text, this duty was extended to *other* male family members as well. This was perhaps on the basis of Leviticus 25:49, where the nearest blood relative had to redeem a person who sold himself as a slave.

In the law of Moses these two compassionate provisions of the Lord were not connected. In the days of the Judges however it had become the custom to do so. It was quite natural to place the levirate duty in connection with the right of redemption, since they often coincided. Now Elimelech had owned a property in Bethlehem (Ruth 4:3). Naomi is trying to sell it, most likely to help take care of her future. Since Boaz was a relative of Elimelech, Naomi hopes and prays that he will not only redeem this piece of land but also marry Ruth. This will perpetuate the family name of Elimelech and Mahlon, Ruth's first husband. It is *this* desire that leads to the events of our chapter. But why have Ruth sneak into Boaz' bed at night? Why not be up front and meet with Boaz during the day and ask him outright?

There are two reasons not to ask Boaz in this manner. First, since Boaz is not a brother of Mahlon, he is not legally bound to marry Ruth. Secondly, another man is a closer relative of Elimelech. He is first in line, but obviously Naomi doesn't fancy him to become Ruth's husband. That's why she uses her feminine wit and ingenuity and sets up this midnight meeting with the fervent hope that Boaz will not refuse to marry her daughter-in-law. Once again, to us it all seems strange and even suspicious. But let's not forget that in the days of the Old Testament the parents played a very important role in arranging the marriage of their children. Let us also not forget that the Lord was pleased to use these events to bring about his purposes. The LORD provides redemption for Elimelech's family in accordance with his Word.

The Plan

With the entry of Boaz into Ruth's life, Naomi becomes a different person. Her concern is no longer about herself and her grief, but about Ruth and her future. She repented from her bitterness and for blaming God for her misfortune and now looks to him with hopeful trust and expectation. When Naomi and Ruth returned to Bethlehem from the land of Moab the future looked grim. A life of poverty seemed to be their lot. But things have changed – the Lord has been so good to them. Naomi has had plenty of time to think. With Ruth away, gleaning at Boaz' farm, she had the days to herself. As she pondered the great changes in their life, and thought about the kindness of the Lord, she looked at the future with different eyes. It doesn't scare her anymore; it starts to look more promising. And that's primarily because of Boaz. The fact that he is one of their kinsman-redeemers doesn't leave her mind. What if Boaz would redeem their property and marry Ruth? Then a whole new future opens up. Then Elimelech's name will continue if the Lord blesses the marriage with children, and Ruth will be well provided for.

And that's why, one day, Naomi decides to act. It's no good waiting for her hopes to come true. There are too many unforeseen circumstances that may prevent her dreams. Harvest time is now over. Ruth no longer goes to work every day. Does that mean that times will get tough again? Naomi loves her daughter-in-law; she'll do anything to help her. And so she says, "My daughter, should I not try to find rest for you, so that it may go well with you?" That's the literal translation of verse 1. Rest, that's what Naomi is after! The rest which God gives and which his Word provides. Naomi had used that word "rest" before in chapter one: when she told Orpah and Ruth to stay in Moab so that they might find rest in the home of another husband. Then she was bitter. and didn't speak from faith. Fancy finding rest in Moab and in a marriage to an unbeliever! That's impossible! True rest can only be found in the Lord. That's why those who marry should marry in the Lord.

Yes, Naomi feels responsible for Ruth, who's been so good to her. Wouldn't it be great if this Moabite girl, who had become a believer in the God of Israel, married in the Lord? And wouldn't Boaz be an ideal husband? Wasn't he a true Israelite who loved God? And doesn't he have the means to take good care of Ruth? Naomi has seen God's guidance, also in the way Boaz has taken a genuine interest in Ruth and how he looked after her as she was gleaning in his fields. He has amply provided for her and Naomi's needs. This is the kind of man who will take God's Word seriously, also when it pertains to the obligations toward the poor and the widows. That's why the rest she craves for Ruth is the rest which a marriage with Boaz will provide. That becomes the most important matter for Naomi. But how to go about it?

No doubt, Naomi spoke to Ruth about her plan and discussed the difficulties they might encounter. The fact that she mentions Boaz again as a kinsman, proves that Ruth knew what that meant, according to the Word of God. But a kinsman could *refuse* to marry a widow. Deuteronomy 25 makes specific mention of that. That is why they must go about it in a careful way. Naomi knows what goes on in the village. She's kept herself up-to-date, especially with regards to Boaz and his work. "Listen Ruth," she says, "tonight he will be winnowing his barley on the threshing floor."

Each village had its own threshing floor which was used by the farmers in turn. As a rule this was done at night, because then the wind was the strongest. The barley would be thrown into the air, and the chaff would blow away while the grain was gathered for storage. The men would not go home but sleep there to protect the precious grain against theft. It was a time of joy, even though it was hard work. The Lord had given his people two feasts that fell within harvest time. The Feast of Weeks and the Feast of Tabernacles. In both cases the Israelites were told to rejoice in God's goodness in providing for their livelihood.

"Well Ruth," says Naomi, "have a bath and put on some nice perfume and dress in your Sunday best. Then go to the threshing floor and wait there until Boaz has eaten and drunk. When he lies down to sleep, you go and uncover his feet and lie down as well. Then you wait. He'll tell you what to do." Ruth agrees to do what Naomi suggests. It's another proof that she's been informed about the plan and knows its purpose. She makes herself ready and leaves for the threshing floor. Once there, she hides herself in the dark and when Boaz finally lies down, at the far end of the grain pile, Ruth sneaks up, cautiously uncovers his feet and lies down as well.

What does all this mean? Why did Naomi devise *this* plan? We said already that Naomi wants Boaz to marry her daughter-in-law, and Ruth is in full agreement with that. But if they wait, if they only *hope* for that marriage, nothing may come of it. Boaz is a busy man. He's got a lot on his mind. Sure, he's been very kind to Ruth and Naomi, but that's no guarantee that he will marry her. That's why Ruth must take the initiative and make herself attractive so Boaz will not refuse to take her as his wife. To us, all this seems very odd. How will Boaz know that this is what Naomi and Ruth are after? Would he not interpret Ruth's behavior as if she was a woman of loose morals, trying to seduce an older man?

That's not case, for the uncovering of Boaz' feet has a special meaning. It is symbolic of a marriage proposal. It is a prelude to what follows in verse nine, when Ruth asks Boaz to spread the corner of his garment over her. That's why Naomi says, "He will tell you what to do." She knows that marriage is the *only* way that Boaz will interpret Ruth's actions. But we are not satisfied yet, are we? Is this acting in faith? Is this a way the Lord approves of? Why not? Does God's providence overrule our responsibility? Is it a proof of faith when we sit back and let things take their own course? No! Faith in the Lord makes us active. It ought to, at least. To remain passive, to trust that God will take care of our life, while refusing to do what we can, is not a sign of faith at all. And that's why we shouldn't fault Naomi and Ruth. Their motives were pure, for they went to God's Word. They read about his provisions for their specific situation. With the family plot up for sale and Elimelech's family name in danger of disappearing, they claimed their covenantal rights, by asking for the redemption which the Lord had promised in his Word.

To us, they go about it in an unorthodox fashion. Considering the circumstances, however, it is understandable. Naomi does not want Ruth to marry just anybody and neither does Ruth want that. Both of them are impressed by Boaz' godliness and compassion. Since he was one of their kinsman-redeemers, he becomes *the* ideal man to provide Ruth with the rest Naomi wishes for her.

Their plan succeeds because the Lord is at work here behind the scenes. He is working out his own purposes which Naomi and Ruth don't know about. He is busy preparing for the coming of his Son, the Redeemer of his church who will liberate his people, not necessarily from poverty but from their bondage to sin. Boaz and Ruth are to play an important part in his coming and that's why Naomi's efforts are blessed. She acts in faith and submits herself and Ruth to the ways of God's Word.

Of course, Naomi has her own hopes as well. She would love to have the security which a marriage between Ruth and Boaz will provide for her. Let's not overreact, as if that is necessarily wrong. Does the Lord frown on such behavior? You don't read that in the Bible. And besides, if we seek to obey God's Word, does that not always bring personal blessings with it? Are God's glory and our wellbeing not the two sides of the gospel of salvation?

The Promise to Secure This Redemption

When in the middle of the night Boaz suddenly wakes up and finds a woman at his feet, he says "Who are you?" Ruth has her answer ready. "I am your servant, Ruth," she says. "Spread the corner of your garment over me, since you are a kinsman-redeemer." This is a direct proposal that Boaz marry her. In Ezekiel 16 we read about the Lord as he marries Israel. In verse 8 we find exactly the same words, as God spreads his garment over his young bride indicating that he takes her for his wife. It's a symbolic pledge of his loving protection. The word for garment can also be translated as "wing". The meaning doesn't change, but it reminds us of what Boaz said to Ruth in chapter two, when he mentioned that she had taken refuge under the wings of Israel's God.

Boaz understands immediately. He's overwhelmed by Ruth's request. He recognizes that she speaks according to God's Word. That's why he calls God's blessing upon her and adds, "This kindness of yours is greater than that you showed before." Ruth's first kindness was her love for her husband

and for Naomi as well, a love that was mainly horizontal. But now she shows it for the Lord and his Word of redemption. She's not a girl who wants to marry at all costs. If that were the case she could have pushed herself on any of the young men of Bethlehem. But Boaz realizes that Ruth seeks a marriage in the Lord. This Moabite girl, this stranger in Israel, has come to faith in Israel's God and she wants to live from that faith. That's why she seeks the redemption of which the law speaks. That's why she turns to Boaz who's been so good to her, and who is their kinsman-redeemer. No doubt, Boaz is quite a bit older than Ruth, as the context makes clear that he isn't a young man anymore. But for Ruth that is a secondary matter. She seeks her future in the way of God's Word. She wants the name of Elimelech's family to continue. She knows by now what that means, for Naomi: offspring who will be alive to welcome the coming Messiah.

It is obvious that Boaz must love Ruth or else he wouldn't speak as he does. His words are full of tenderness and feeling. He's struck by this girl, as are others. "All the townsfolk know that you are a woman of noble character," he says. Ruth is not a flirt, much less a loose woman. She loves the Lord and that is why she agrees to Naomi's plan. Boaz understands and he doesn't waste any time either. "Don't worry, my daughter. I will do what you're asking," he says. He doesn't promise, "I will marry you." He couldn't say that because there was another man, a closer relative, who had the first obligation to do so. But Boaz promises that he will do whatever must be done to assure Ruth of the redemption she's seeking.

Once again, his words show us that Boaz is a god-fearing man. We don't know *how much* he already loved Ruth, but he doesn't take matters in his own hand. He submits himself to the Word of God. That's where the answer must come from. In his loving care for this young widow, who by God's grace became a member of his church and a believing child, Boaz recognizes his responsibility. He truly is his sister's keeper. "Stay here for the night," he says, "and if that other, that closer relative will redeem you, so be it. But if not, I promise you by the name of God that I will do it. Just remain here till the morning." Do you see that Boaz gives precedence to the Word of God? He is not determined to marry Ruth, come what may, but he lets the Scriptures speak. His personal desires become secondary to what the Lord reveals.

Boaz submitted to the Word because he was a man of faith. All of God's children ought to be like this. A lot of progress has happened in redemptive history from the time of Boaz to our time. Nevertheless, the principles by which Boaz lived must also be our principles. He enjoyed God's redemption and spoke of it to others. To do that, we must first listen very carefully to what God's Word tells us. Then submit to it. For God's redemption, whether in the Old or New Testament, is based on his Word. If we take shortcuts with that Word, if we try to assure our future by following our own desires (even when they are religious), nothing will come of it. That's why Boaz' promise carried so much weight. He spoke and acted according to God's Word and when you do that, you may trust that all will be well.

That's what Ruth does! She trusts this man. She doesn't get upset that someone else might redeem and marry her but surrenders herself to the will of the Lord. Sure, she craves the redemption of Elimelech's family, and she fervently hopes that Boaz won't refuse to take her as his wife. However, when she hears his answer, she understands that the Word of God must be obeyed. Ruth may have been a recent convert, but she certainly shows her trust in Israel's God, who has been so good to her and Naomi. In so many ways she has tasted his love for her - once a stranger. He will also care for her in the future. Does his Word not assure her of that? Are its stipulations that deal with redemption not given to guarantee her and her mother-in-law that all will turn out well?

Boaz can't send Ruth home immediately. It is dark and the town's gates are closed during the night; they don't want any gossip either. That's why Ruth gets up early to slip back into the village. Boaz doesn't want her to go emptyhanded. He realizes that there's much at stake for this girl. Sure, she trusts him and agrees that the redemption they seek is prescribed in God's law. But that doesn't mean that it's always easy. That's why he gives her six measures of barley. It's a going-away present for Ruth and Naomi. A proof of his love for this girl and a further assurance that he will do all he can to bring the matter to a satisfactory end. Then Boaz himself also sets out for Bethlehem. His mind is busy with one thing: the redemption of Naomi and Ruth. He won't rest until that is settled.

Beautiful! Here Boaz foreshadows Jesus Christ. Did he not desire to do his Father's will? Was he not keen to redeem his people and marry his church?

It's true that the redemption of which Ruth 3 speaks and the redemption which Christ accomplished are not remotely the same, but they have this in common: both of them could only be achieved by a believing submission to the Word of God. Both of them demand that not just anyone, but the nearest kinsman-redeemer undertake it. That's why Christ had to become one of us. That's why he wasn't ashamed to call us his brothers. That's why Christmas became a divine necessity. Rather than a romantic event where feelings and emotions prevailed, it was the beginning of our Lord's humiliation, where he identified himself completely with us sinners. He was willing to leave his divine glory behind and share our existence with all its sorrows, fears, and agonies, as our kinsman-Redeemer!

Patience to Wait

Naomi probably didn't sleep very well - her thoughts would have been with Ruth. When she hears footsteps she can't wait. "How did it go my daughter?" she asks. Then Ruth tells her everything that transpired during the night. The best news she has for Naomi is that Boaz has sworn to fulfill the duty of redemption if the nearest kinsman-redeemer isn't interested. It's *that* promise, that willingness to do all that Naomi and Ruth ask, which fills Ruth with joy. The fact she received six measures of barley underlines that willingness. That also tells Naomi that Boaz is aware of his God-given obligation to spread his wings, not only over Ruth but also over Naomi and her property.

That's why Naomi says, "Wait my daughter, until you find out what happens. For this Boaz, this God-fearing man will not rest until the matter is settled today." Do you hear how Naomi reacts in trusting faith? What a difference from her former attitude, when she was bitter and blamed the Lord for all that had happened. But now, she counsels Ruth to wait. That also means that *she* has to wait. Don't be cynical and say: "What else could they do?" This waiting is a fruit of faith. If there is no faith, if people feel the Lord has short changed them, if they go through life with bitter feelings and blame everyone else but themselves, then they don't wait. Then they take matters in their own hands. Then they force their own will through, and don't care how they go about it. Even if they can't do anything about the situation and they are completely dependent on others, they still don't wait. They become rebellious and start to complain and accuse.

That's why Naomi's advice can only be explained by her faith. She believes that the Lord will make everything well. Waiting is terribly hard. Waiting for the Lord to act doesn't come naturally, not for Naomi and Ruth, and not for you and me. Yet God's time is always the best time. He doesn't let his children wait unnecessarily; he keeps his promises in his specific time. Look at the history of redemption. See how many centuries elapsed before it became Christmas. Yet the Bible tells us that it was precisely "when the time had fully come, that God sent his Son, born of a woman and born under the law, to redeem those under law, that we might receive the full rights of sons" (Galatians 4:4-5). When the time had *fully* come. Not a week too early, not a day too late.

That's why Naomi's waiting is a waiting in faith. She is certain that the Lord will take care of them. Not in the way we want, preferably instantaneous, but at God's time and in the way of his Word. Here we see that this elderly woman is not a scheming mother-in-law whose desires go no further than her personal wishes. She's not upset either that another man may ruin what she would love to see: to have Boaz redeem their property and marry Ruth and so continue Elimelech's family and assure it of a new future.

Are we able to wait in this manner? Oh, our circumstances are completely different than that of our text. The ceremonial laws of redeeming properties and marrying a brother's widow no longer apply. Christ has come and has fulfilled all the laws which were only poor shadows of what God's covenantal compassion stands for. His great love and profound mercy and wonderful grace can be seen in the perfect redemption which he accomplished on the cross. He didn't set us free with gold and silver but with his precious blood. That's why he had to be made *like* us, except without sin. That's why we are of the same family (Hebrews 2:11), so that he could become our kinsman-Redeemer. He freed us body and soul, from all our enemies and assures us of a future that is simply too glorious to imagine.

This is the wonderful truth of the gospel and it applies to all who believe. But that's not all. For we are still living on this earth, where the horrors of sin spawn so much pain, fear and agony. This creation is still held in bondage and we're still faced with every kind of danger and threat. Violence and persecution, terminal illness and approaching death, sorrow and tears, pain and fears are not strange to us. But we have the Word of our God, the gospel of Jesus Christ. We have his promise that all will turn out well. That is why we wait - not with bowed heads, wondering what's going to happen, but with eagerness and trust. Our God will not disappoint us. The Day will surely come when also the earth will be set free from its bondage to decay. The wedding of Christ and his bride is rapidly approaching and we will be completely redeemed. Then the fruits of God's redemption will be perfectly enjoyed. Then death will be no more, neither mourning or crying or pain. Then God will wipe every tear from our eyes. Then we will live with him, completely taken under the shelter of his wings, perfectly at peace in the bosom of our bridegroom.

Questions

1. Naomi and Ruth's plan to go to Boaz at night is "acting in faith". Give 2 examples of how we might "act in faith".

   What do the words, "As it turned out…" in Ruth 2:3 imply?

2. Is there ever a time to "sit back and let things take their course"?

3. What is the most important factor to consider when deciding to do something life-changing like Ruth did?

4. It seems that in this chapter "the end justifies the means", because the desired outcome was godly. Is this an accurate interpretation of Naomi's plan? Does the end *ever* justify the means?

5. What is the significance to Ruth that Boaz spread his garment over her?

6. How does Boaz secure Ruth's trust in him?

7. How does Ruth show her trust in Israel's (now her) God?

8. What characteristics does this chapter hint are important to look for in a godly husband?

What characteristics would be important to look for in a godly wife?

Are these characteristics only important to have if you intend to marry?

9. Patience is a fruit of the Spirit. We see both Ruth and Naomi waiting on the LORD. Is patience something we can get better at? How?

Describe the attitude and actions of "patient waiting." Give some examples of what "patient waiting" is *not*.

What if what we are waiting for never comes? (ie: new job, spouse, baby, good health)

What promises from the LORD can we hold on to as we wait? Provide Bible texts.

48

Ruth 4

The Glorious Messianic Future

Additional Reading: Deuteronomy 28:1-14

Suggested singing: Psalm 25:10; Hymn 67:1,2,6

At Christmas we remember that God sent his son into this world to redeem his people from their sins; to purchase for himself a church chosen to life eternal. Christ came to usher in the kingdom of heaven, where everything will be restored to a life where God in Jesus Christ will be loved and served for his great love and marvelous grace. That's why the angel told Mary that "the Lord God will give [Jesus] the throne of his father David, and he will reign over the house of Jacob forever; his kingdom will never end." (Luke 1:32-33) That's why Nathanael, one of his first disciples exclaimed by the Holy Spirit: "You are the Son of God; you are the King of Israel" (John 1:49). And that's also why the majority of the Jews rejected him, when they said to Pilate, "This man claims to be King... But we have no king but Caesar!" (John 19:12,15)

All of this provides us with ample evidence that Jesus Christ came to this world as the God-ordained Messiah. He was prophet, priest, and king. As Prophet he made known to us the way of salvation, like no one else. As Priest, he sacrificed himself for our sins. And as King, he came to deliver us from all our enemies and to reign forever in a kingdom of peace and righteousness. It is Christ's kingship that has the main attention in the book of Ruth. You don't recognize that when you just skim over its pages. Then the book of Ruth seems to be a short novel with a sad beginning and a happy end; where you meet ordinary people with their joys and griefs. If you don't look any further, you'll miss the deeper meaning of this part of

God's holy Word. Then you won't understand the family tree at the end of this chapter and will fail to see what the Lord is busy with in and through the events that are related here. Yes, ordinary events. Things that happened more often in the lives of many other Jews – becoming widowed; being poor; a promising marriage and the birth of a child.

The happenings that are related in the chapters of Ruth are part of redemptive history. They reveal that the Lord is busy preparing for the coming of Christ, who is born as the son of David. He is the legitimate heir to the throne. Christ's kingship is totally different than what we normally witness. He wasn't born in a palace but in a stable. He didn't deliver his people by means of the sword but with his blood. He came to set us free from our greatest enemy, which is sin. That could only be achieved when he died the death we deserve. He then rose from the dead and is now seated at the right hand of God, not only to preserve his church against the attacks of the devil, but also to prepare for his return. He will appear in glory to take his people to himself and let them enjoy the blessings of his kingdom where peace and righteousness rule. He will also return to destroy his adversaries, defeating the kingdom of darkness by consigning all his and our enemies to their eternal doom.

It will be a long and arduous path, for a lot has to happen. When the book of Ruth was written, some 1000 years before Christmas, very little was revealed to the people of God. Today we know much, much more. Back then, information was given via symbols and shadows. God's church was spoon fed, you might say, a little bit at a time. But that was enough! They wouldn't have understood everything, anyhow. What they needed to know was not withheld from them. What did the Lord assure them of with this book? He assured them of his redemption. He made it clear to them that the promise of a coming king would be fulfilled, via the tribe of Judah, as Jacob had prophesied: "The scepter will not depart from Judah" (Genesis 49:10). That is the deeper meaning of the events of chapter 4. That is also the gospel promise in the redemption of Elimelech's family: that the Lord assures his people of the coming of a glorious Messianic future.

Redemption Refused
Boaz doesn't waste any time. He's convinced that Naomi and Ruth must be helped according to the provisions of God's law. He heads for the gate

of Bethlehem, where all important matters take place, where transactions are discussed and legal proceedings dealt with. It doesn't take long before the kinsman-redeemer comes into sight. Providentially, the Lord makes sure that the redemption of Elimelech's family could proceed without delay. "Please, sit down for a while," says Boaz. "We've got some important business to attend to." The man obliges. Before Boaz comes with his proposition, though, he gathers ten of the town's elders to function as witnesses. Life was not as complicated as it is now – professional lawyers did not exist, nor imposing court buildings. Most of the business that needed to be dealt with was done orally. Legality was very important though, so every far-reaching matter had to be witnessed to give it legitimacy.

When the ten witnesses have also taken their seat, Boaz says to the kinsman-redeemer:

> No doubt, you know about Naomi. She has recently returned from Moab and since she is poor, she is obliged to sell the piece of land that belonged to her husband, Elimelech. *You* happen to be her nearest relative, so I thought to bring this matter to your attention. Why don't you redeem the land and so preserve Elimelech's inheritance in Israel? That's why I asked these witnesses to be present. If you're willing, please do so but if not, let me know. You have the first right of redemption. Not me! I'm second in line.

The kinsman-redeemer does not hesitate. "I will redeem it." But then Boaz brings up a matter which is closely tied to the redemption of Elimelech's plot of land. "If you're willing to redeem the property that now belongs to Naomi and her daughter-in-law, you must also take Ruth to wife so that the family name of Elimelech is maintained and does not become extinct in Israel." At this the kinsman-redeemer has a sudden change of mind. "No," he says, "I can't do that! For then I may endanger my own estate. Why don't you redeem it? I can't do it anymore."

What causes this sudden change? Why was the man willing to redeem the property but unwilling to marry Ruth? What does he exactly mean that he might "endanger his own estate"? The commentaries are not unanimous. Some claim that his excuse is not valid at all, for if he marries Ruth and the marriage remains childless, the field will remain in his name. On the other hand, if he has a child with her, the child will *also* be *his* son or daughter.

And the property will therefore stay in his family all the same. Others suggest that the man is probably *already* married and has children. That's why he is afraid that if he marries Ruth and has more children, it will cause jealousy and animosity in his family, especially when it comes to dividing his inheritance. The Bible is quiet here. It doesn't tell us how and why a marriage with Ruth would jeopardize the man's own estate. So we better keep quiet as well and refrain from speculation.

One thing becomes very clear: this kinsman-redeemer doesn't show any compassion or love toward Naomi and Ruth. He doesn't mind redeeming the real estate. Assuring the continuation of Elimelech's family by marrying his daughter-in-law is another matter. This man is not obliged by law to do what Boaz asks, as he is not a brother of Mahlon and Kilion. But what about the *spirit* of the law? What about God's will that his people do what they could to prevent any of Israel's families from becoming extinct, so they could then welcome the promised Messiah? What about being concerned with Naomi and Ruth, who humanly speaking faced a dark future because of their widowhood? That allows us a glimpse into this man's heart, where genuine interest and the willingness to sacrifice was sadly missing.

How different Jesus Christ was, when he came to redeem his church. Was he concerned that it might endanger his own position? Was he unwilling to sacrifice? On the contrary! He volunteered to liberate his people. "He left his glory in heaven and made himself nothing," says Paul in Philippians 2:7, "taking the very nature of a servant." He came and he stood right next to us, sinners. He was filled with compassion and love. He didn't only stick to the letter of the law! Instead, Christ became our brother so that he could be our kinsman-redeemer. That's why Christmas was necessary. Christ had one desire: to marry his church! Not because she was beautiful, but because he loved her, despite all her sins and iniquities. He came to redeem her so that she might enjoy the freedom of the children of God. He wanted her to share the inheritance that was his: the new heavens and the new earth and the security that comes with it, and to live forever in the peace and joy that is found under his wings.

The unnamed kinsman-redeemer of our chapter reminds us of the New Testament Pharisees and many others since. Very precise with the letter but totally devoid of the spirit of God's law. Religious? You better believe it! But no care, no love, no compassion for God's people, their brothers and sisters. When it came to the point, they were only concerned about themselves. That's why they had no time for the poor and the lonely, the widows and the orphans, the vulnerable and the weak. They ill-treated them and used them for their own advantage. No wonder Christ had no good word for them, but exposed their religiosity as hypocritical and absolutely worthless in the sight of God.

Ruth 4:8 reminds us that the book of Ruth was written well after the events took place. The custom to take off your sandal and to give it to someone else was no longer practiced by then. At the time it symbolized the official transfer of your rights. In this case, the right of redemption. Perhaps it originated from the fact that walking on a piece of land, implied ownership. The sandal or shoe symbolized the authority of possession. In Psalm 60:8, for example, the Lord himself makes use of this symbolism when he says, "Upon Edom I toss my sandal". That's another way of saying: Edom belongs to me. That's why the kinsman-redeemer takes off his sandal and gives it to Boaz. Redemption is a public matter that must be witnessed to make it legitimate and that includes the transfer of that right to someone else. That's what happens here. Boaz now becomes the person who is officially and lawfully designated as the redeemer of Elimelech's family. Boaz doesn't shirk this God-given responsibility but accepts it willingly.

Redemption Realized!

If the first kinsman-redeemer reveals something of the attitude of the later Pharisees, Boaz shows the mind of Jesus Christ. He doesn't waste time by asking himself how to avoid this situation. He's not only concerned with the letter of the law but is motivated by a deep desire to fulfill its spirit. There's an Israelite family at the brink of extinction! There are two widows whose future looks grim, humanly speaking! For if nothing happens, if no kinsman is willing to redeem Elimelech's family, there will be no offspring to welcome the Messiah. That was a terrible thing for a Jewish family. They longed to have their family present at the glorious coming of Israel's Redeemer/King, who would deliver them, not from temporal afflictions first of all, but from their sin and its eternal misery. He would not be concerned about a plot of land in an earthly Canaan but assured them of an everlasting inheritance in the new creation. He would marry his church, not for some 30 or 50 years, but for ever and ever. Loving her with all the love of his heart so that she would be taken care of in a way she can't even begin to imagine.

This desire to serve is reflected by Boaz. By now he has come to love Ruth. Ever since he got to know her, he was captivated by her commitment to Naomi and her love for Israel's God. When, in the previous chapter, she proposed that he redeem Elimelech's family and marry her, Boaz' promise to do what he could was not devoid of his personal desire to take this girl as his wife. In *that* regard, the love of Christ for his church is completely different. We didn't endear ourselves to him. There was nothing that attracted him to us. On the contrary, it was pure grace and divine love – something we will never understand and which ought to make us more thankful for the redemption he purchased with the price of his life.

Boaz now calls on the elders and all the others who had stopped by to watch the proceedings and he solemnly declares that they are witnesses of what transpires here. "I have purchased (for that's what redemption is, it always comes at a price) all the property of Elimelech, Kilion and Mahlon. That also means that I will marry Ruth, the widow of Mahlon." And then he gives the reason! The main reason! The same reason he mentioned to that first kinsman in verse 5; so that Elimelech's name, via his daughter-in-law, will not disappear from his family and town.

All the people present, answer in unison: "Yes, we are witnesses!" They also call on God to give his blessing on this marriage. "May Ruth be like Rachel and Leah, who together built up the house of Israel and may Boaz become a man of standing in Ephrathah and famous in Bethlehem." Even more than he already was! And then they add, "May your family be like that of Perez whom Tamar bore to Judah, through the offspring which the Lord gives you by this young woman."

We often have our questions as to how deep the faith of Israel went. More than once, when we read the Old Testament we wonder how much they understood of God's promises and how much they cherished them in their daily life. We said it already: they were people of their time. They lived at the beginning of God's covenant with Abraham and his descendants. They had no Bibles to consult like we have. They couldn't just flip a few pages and read with their own eyes what exactly the Lord had foretold and how exactly his promises were to be fulfilled. Does that mean they were foreign to the faith? Must we presume that the Lord and his gospel meant very little to them? No. There were many who loved God and treasured his promises. They didn't have them written down, at least, not so that each had his own copy. But at the tabernacle the priests would remind them of God's promises. And the parents would pass on the great deeds of God in Israel's history from generation to generation. Doesn't that become clear from our text? How else would they have known about Rachel and Leah who were mothers in Israel, whom God used to build his Old Testament church by giving them a large offspring?

Why was Perez, the oldest son of Judah and his daughter-in-law Tamar mentioned? Because it was Perez who was chosen by God to be the forefather of David and Jesus Christ. Not Zerah, his younger brother, nor Shelah, Judah's oldest surviving son who was the uncle of Perez. It's true, the people at that time did not know that yet. They were ignorant as to which line of Judah the Messiah would be born from. Therefore Perez' name is mentioned primarily because Boaz was a descendant of his. But that takes nothing away from what we said about the prophecy of the blessing. Don't forget, when these words were written, time had moved on quite a few years. The author of this little book lived at least during the time of King David, if not later. And that's why the words of blessing, spoken by the people of Bethlehem have prophetic significance.

God had these blessings written down, not only for Boaz' and Ruth's sake, but for all who would come after them as well. That includes us. He assures his church of all times that the blessings of Ruth 4:11,12 are not only for that situation, but apply to the church of all times and places. God's covenant promises are not limited to forgiveness and reconciliation, as symbolized by the sacrifices that were brought at the tabernacle. Read Deuteronomy 28. Does it apply here? Very much!

In our times the gospel centres around the birth, crucifixion, and resurrection of Jesus Christ. Don't misunderstand that, these are the true and glorious redemptive events that secured our salvation. No one who doesn't believe them will be saved. But the danger we are facing is that we restrict God's redemption in Christ to these facts. That we spiritualize the gospel. That we lose sight of *all* that belongs to it. For Christ did not only reconcile us to God through his blood. He doesn't only assure the believers that their soul is safe when they die. Rather, he came to renew our whole existence. God's promise of salvation assures us of a life that abounds in every possible way. That's why God's Old Testament church was assured of prosperity and abundance, of many children and a renowned name. I know, things have changed. In the New Testament dispensation these promises and blessings are no longer in force, at least not to the same extent. The church of Christ often suffers. Many believers are treated as nobodies and worse. But let's not forget that this is only temporary! Let us not disregard these blessings of the Lord as if they have served their time.

The redemption that God has promised and which is foreshadowed in our text will not only liberate us from hopelessness and despair and assure us of a safe place under the wings of God's great love and compassion, but in due time it will exalt our whole existence. That's why the Bible speaks of believers reigning as kings with Christ and of the nations that will bring their treasures into the New Jerusalem. That is what is symbolized and foreshadowed by our text. The people of Bethlehem who recognize that Boaz lives by faith and therefore redeemed Elimelech's family by marrying Ruth, now wish him the promises God has enjoined to such faith. The blessing of children and a place of honour. Not an honour that is the result of personal scheming and ruthless egoism, but an honour that comes as God's reward on a life of faith.

What a difference with our times, where children are aborted and small families are the norm. Where honour is often given to those who glory in their shame, rather than in the grace of God. Boaz, a God-fearing Israelite, reveals something of the spirit of Jesus Christ. By assuring the continuation of Elimelech's family, he prefigures the Messiah who came to realize the redemption of all who turn to him in faith. He didn't redeem us with gold and with silver, but with his own blood, that colossal price which sets us free from our bondage to sin. So he assures us of a future that will reach a height and a fullness we can't even begin to understand. That's right: us. But a better way would be: Christ's family. All his children. An innumerable multitude. No wonder the Bible gives to Christ a name of great renown. It's the Name above every other name! Not only in Ephrathah of Judah and in Bethlehem where he was born, but a name before which every knee shall bow - wherever they live, even in the most remote corners of the earth.

Did Boaz, Ruth and Naomi see any of the blessings which this redemption contained? Did the people of Bethlehem see them? Do we, as we read this little book? Yes, and in this way that redemption is revealed.

How This Redemption is Revealed

It doesn't take long and the wedding is celebrated. The Lord blesses their marriage and Ruth becomes the mother of a little boy. The women of the town pay Naomi a visit and congratulate her with her grandson. They praise the Lord for this precious gift. Now she has her own kinsman-redeemer: a *Goel*! A man who will in due time take care of her and defend her. For that role belongs to the *Goel* or Redeemer. The word is also applied to the person who sticks up for his relatives and defends them and even avenges them. That's why Jeremiah calls God the *Goel* of his people: he who is strong and will vigorously defend their cause. And Isaiah speaks of God as the Almighty *Goel*! It's important to remember that, also when we think of the redemption that Christ has accomplished on behalf of his church. That does not only mean that he liberated us from the power of sin and curse but it includes his daily care for us and defending us against all our enemies. He will destroy them eventually.

Boaz and Ruth now recede into the background and Naomi comes to the fore again. That's because the redemption has to do with her family, first of all. It's in this little boy, who receives the name Obed (which means "servant"), that Naomi sees and experiences the faithfulness and grace of the Lord. Instead of disappearing from the people of Israel, Obed assures this elderly widow that in and through him, Elimelech's family will not miss out on the Messianic future. How Naomi is reminded of the great love of God! What a difference we witness in her attitude. Once bitter and blaming the Lord for all her troubles, she must have been dumb struck by the mysterious ways of the Lord. He brought her daughter-in-law, a Moabite girl, to Canaan to care for and look after her. He worked faith in Ruth's heart. She didn't marry just anyone but sought the redemption which God's law prescribed. She was just as concerned as her mother-in-law about the future of the family. The women of Bethlehem understood that too. All that happened to Naomi and Ruth has been used by God for their good and all of it is a result of his redemption as spelled out in his Word.

That's why Naomi is overwhelmed by God's goodness. She can't be kept away from little Obed. She makes it her task to look after him. Ruth most likely has a lot of work to attend to as the wife of a successful farmer. Naomi's help comes in very handy. And Ruth has no concerns about how her mother-in-law will raise him. Too much has happened – the grace of God had been demonstrated to them in so many ways. What else could Naomi do but show her thankfulness by nurturing the boy in the ways of the Lord? Obed! Servant! What a prophetic name! The townsfolk have no trouble recognizing that. They have no clue of the wider importance of that name, though. They must have thought of Boaz, how he served his God by redeeming this family and that the name "Obed" was chosen because the parents wished the little boy would serve his grandmother just as much.

For us who have seen how the Lord continued to use this family for the coming of the Messiah, this name receives a far deeper meaning. Also the author of this book already sees far more than the people of Bethlehem. That's why he adds that family tree. It almost looks like an afterthought. It isn't, though, for this genealogy provides us with the key to understanding this little book. Without it we wouldn't really know what God was working toward by means of these events. Ten generations are mentioned. Now we see that it was from the line of Perez that the Christ would be born! Sure, his name isn't mentioned yet. It only goes to David, another servant of the Lord. He was the king used by God to liberate his people from the yoke of their enemies. It was under David that the Promised Land reached its widest borders. And it was David who unified the nation under God's Word. And it was David again, who through his many psalms comforted God's people – not in the least with the promise that one day the Messiah would come, as his great Son, whose kingdom would have no end and who would reign over all.

See how God kept working toward the Messianic future? See how he used the people mentioned in this book? See that the author understood the significance of this redemption as it opened the way to the throne of David? See what we now know, that the promised Messiah hailed from this family tree? Jesus Christ - the New Testament Obed! The perfect fulfilment of what his forefather's name stood for! How often does the Bible not mention that Christ is the servant of God? And did he not prove himself to be the complete Redeemer of all who turn to him? Who cares for his people like Jesus? Who looks after his brothers and sisters like Christ? Does it surprise us that the Bible says that he came not to be served but to serve and to give his life as a ransom for many? He lifts up the humble and fills the hungry with good things. But he scatters those who are proud and brings rulers down from their thrones. That's what his mother Mary already said before he was born. How much more have we seen the truth of those words?

Therefore, let us boast in the name of our covenant God, who fulfils all he has promised. Let us glory in Jesus Christ, the great son of David, as our Redeemer and King. Let us do that, not just in church but as we live our life in this world full of problems and tensions. A world where sin and evil continue to escalate.

Yes, let us boast from the certainty of faith! Looking forward with eager anticipation to the day our full redemption will be revealed. Oh, we often wonder about the future and we are fearful for what our children and grandchildren may have to go through; when we see wickedness increasing and godlessness mushroom. But let us then listen to our *Goel*, Jesus Christ who told his church in Luke 21:28, "When you see these things taking place, stand up and lift up your head, because your redemption is drawing near." *Your* redemption! *Your* full and glorious salvation! And that's why we end this study with the prayer: Lord, come quickly.

Questions

1. Why did Boaz not agree to redeem Ruth immediately?

2. How does the response of the kinsman-redeemer change once he learns he will receive a wife, too?

Can we judge his answer?

3. Contrast the unnamed kinsman-redeemer with Jesus.

4. Give two examples of how we as a church (and individuals) still fall into the same sin as the kinsman-redeemer.

5. What did people in Bethlehem understand of God's plan to redeem his people?

   Do you think that understanding caused them to value large families more than we do today?

   Read Deuteronomy 28. What does that have to do with Ruth 4?

6. Reread the eighth paragraph under the heading "Redemption Realized". We read that Christians today may restrict God's redemption in Christ to his birth, death and resurrection, and so "spiritualize the gospel". What does this mean?

___

How does Christ exalt our whole existence?

___

Does God promise in these passages to grant believing Christians children, honour and wealth? Provide proof texts for your position.

___

7. Is redemption "completely" revealed to Boaz and Ruth or only partially?

___

8. Boaz redeems Elimelech's family from extinction. What is the connection between Obed's name and the name of Christ?

___

9. Read Luke 1:46-55, which is commonly called "Mary's Song". What does she prophecy about Jesus' life?

___

What is our "full" redemption? (Read Luke 21:28.)

_____
_____
_____

What is the day of redemption (Ephesians 4:30)?

_____
_____
_____
_____
_____

Prayer before your Bible study

Gracious God and Father, we thank you that you have gathered us as your people here in study. Here it pleases you to be in our midst, closer than anywhere else. Here you come to us with all the blessings of salvation which your Holy Spirit is pleased to distribute through the means of grace. It is by means of the gospel, that power unto salvation for everyone who believes, that you bring us to faith and strengthen us in that faith. And that's what we stand in need of, Lord! We can't live without your gospel. For without the gospel of redemption our life remains under the yoke of our sins and the curse of your wrath. Without your forgiveness we will never find peace and we remain strangers to the joy that is reserved for those who surrender themselves to Jesus Christ, the only Name given under heaven by which we must be saved.

And that's why we thank you Father for your grace and mercies. That's why we are so blessed to belong to your covenant people. And that's why coming together to study you is not a "must" first of all, but a privilege. Where we may meet with you, our covenant God and loving Father. To worship you. To lift up your holy name in our songs and prayers. And to ascribe to you all glory, honour and praise for the redemption that you accomplished in your son Jesus Christ. Lord, be merciful to us. Do not deal with us as we deserve. Wash away all our sins and create in us a heart that loves and serves you. So that we live in thankful obedience to your commandments.

Bless us therefore through this Bible study here. Strengthen us that we may do that faithfully, clearly, and boldly. Open our hearts to receive it with joy. To live from it in our day to day life. Lord, you know how the struggle against sin can make us so tired. You know how often we go down to defeat. You know how very small our obedience is. How often we fail you and each other. How even our best works are contaminated with sin and fall so far short from the perfection that you require. Look at us in and through your son Jesus Christ. Cover us with his righteousness and holiness. Fill us with your Holy Spirit so that we don't become discouraged but live from the strength he provides. Remind us that your love never fails. That you hold on to us and will bring us to the day our redemption will be perfect and glorious.

May we live as a light in this dark world. May others be blessed through our words and actions. May we display to all people that the gospel of Jesus Christ is the only message that redeems us from sin and all its terrible consequences and gives us a peace that passes all understanding. May that gospel also be heard when we turn to the Old Testament, which is also full of Jesus Christ and where your covenant faithfulness provides us with much comfort. It assures us that you will fulfil all you have promised, because of Christ, our one and only Redeemer. Hear our prayer Lord, in his name alone.

Amen.

Prayer after your Bible study

Merciful God and Father, we thank you for the gospel of redemption! We praise you for your grace and love. That you had compassion on us, sinners in and through the suffering and death of our Lord Jesus Christ, who is our one and only redeemer, our *Goel*, who liberates us from the shackles of sin and the miseries that come in its wake. He assures us of an inheritance that is kept in heaven for us and that can never perish, spoil, or fade, and will be our eternal home. A home where your church may dwell with Christ who redeemed and married her to let her live under the safety of his wings for ever and ever.

We saw a little of that when we heard the gospel in the book of Ruth. How you, as the covenant God of your people Israel, not only promised them the full redemption from all their enemies, but also foreshadowed and prefigured that in this part of your Word. You kept the future open, Lord! The future that led to the throne of David. And in due time to his great son Jesus Christ who would reign over the house of Israel for ever. You encouraged not only Naomi and Ruth but all the people of Bethlehem, that your promises will be fulfilled. And we have seen that fulfilment Father! We have witnessed what none of your Old Testament people ever saw: that in your Son you came to redeem sinners. That he gave his own life as a ransom for many. That he continues to love and care for her and at his time will bring her home to be with him for ever!

Father in heaven, we thank you for this wonderful news. And for the great blessing that we may share in it. Share in it by faith. A faith that also shows up, by wanting to walk in the way of your commandments. Bless us as congregation. May the spirit of Jesus Christ make us humble and willing to serve. May we help and encourage each other as we travel forward to the day of Christ. May we look forward to that day with eager longing.

Lord, be with your people all across this world. Bless the faithful proclamation of the gospel for the salvation of many. Strengthen all your servants and that includes those who work on the mission field, that also through their labours your kingdom may come and your people be established in the faith.

We pray for the many of our brothers and sisters who suffer so much for the name of Christ. Hold on to them in your love, Father, and give them the grace to persevere. May through their sufferings your name be hallowed and their adversaries brought to their knees, when they witness how your love enables your children to remain faithful unto death. Lord, as yet we must live by faith and we do not see the full redemption which Christ has accomplished. As yet, so many of your children are treated with contempt, hatred, and violence. May your kingdom soon arrive. Rend the heavens, Father, and prove yourself to be the Redeemer of all who trust in you. Then you will not only glorify all your children by granting them the full redemption of body and soul but also destroy all of his and our enemies. May that hope soften all our sorrow and spur us on to live close to you. That's what we pray, in the name of Christ. Our Redeemer!

Amen.

www.ingramcontent.com/pod-product-compliance
Lightning Source LLC
Chambersburg PA
CBHW072109290426
44110CB00014B/1874